My Zócalo Heart

poems by

Mary E. Torregrossa

Finishing Line Press
Georgetown, Kentucky

My Zócalo Heart

Copyright © 2018 by Mary E. Torregrossa
ISBN 978-1-63534-358-8 First Edition
All rights reserved under International and Pan-American Copyright Conventions.
No part of this book may be reproduced in any manner whatsoever without written permission from the publisher, except in the case of brief quotations embodied in critical articles and reviews.

ACKNOWLEDGMENTS

Thank you to the following publications where these poems first appeared or were recognized:

Writers at Work poem of the month, "In the Canyon of Beauty and Lament"
Los Angeles Poetry Society 2013 poetry contest, "Sister Sun"
East Jasmine Review, "Undedicated Street" and "A Bullet In His Head"
Poetry In The Windows Vl, Arroyo Arts Collective, "Day Laborer" in Spanish and English
Wide Awake—Poetry of Los Angeles and Beyond, Pacific Coast Poetry Series, "Our Cemetery"

For their comments, readings and support, thanks to Deborah Fiedler Apraku, Jack and Annie Laurie Babson, Don Campbell, Lorenzo Contreras, Katerina Canyon, Anne Babson Carter, Consuelo Flores, June Inuzuku, Joe Kelly, Ron Koertge, Elaine Loarca, Penelope Moffet, Osvaldo Navarro, Toti OBrien, Carl Stillwell, Morgan Zo, and to Jennifer Shultz Mitchell for help with translation.

Publisher: Leah Maines

Editor: Christen Kincaid

Cover Art: photographer Enrico Sortino and graphic artist Sean Boes

Author Photo: Nina A. Loarca

Cover Design: Elizabeth Maines McCleavy

Printed in the USA on acid-free paper.
Order online: www.finishinglinepress.com
also available on amazon.com

Author inquiries and mail orders:
Finishing Line Press
P. O. Box 1626
Georgetown, Kentucky 40324
U. S. A.

Table of Contents

In The Canyon Of Beauty And Lament 1
Détente 2
The Box That Is Night 3
Picking Mushrooms 4
Sister Sun 5
Father On The Staircase 6
The Summer Tree 8
Pool Play 9
Meeting Safira 10
At The Zócalo 11
La Fuente Dulce 12
Her Earrings 13
Night Thyme 14
Bus Route After The Fires 15
Undedicated Street 16
Avvoltoi 17
Angel's Mother 18
Nixtamal 19
Desert Crossing 20
Day Laborer 21
Selling Candy 22
Uncle Lowell And His Niece Play Hide And Secret 23
Rendezvous 24
Neighbors 25
Old Dogs 26
The Bullet In His Head 27
Our Cemetery 28

For my husband Mynor L. Loarca

In The Canyon Of Beauty And Lament
for poet Denise Chávez

Red cliffs never smile,
the air is rarely still
even on the calmest days.
At night, the cottonwood
leaves wave frantically.

Here I do not deeply sleep.
Here the spirits move
in fragile gales,
an ebony horse flies across
the indigo bridge of sky.

All the birds and beetles
hide. At sunrise the tops
of pine trees warble.
I envy them their song.

Détente

This might be my remedy
this amber signature of tea
set here before us in cups
of glass too hot to touch.
The scent of steeping
mint leaves drifts
redolent in my thoughts.
Like an aftershock
of the Sierra Madre,
I rattle silver teaspoons
into saucers, sit
clenching sugar cubes
in my back teeth
like Esther, or Kobra,
or Zahra might have
years ago or yesterday.
The tonic eases its way
into your explanation
infused with details
of the truth. I listen,
waiting for the tea to cool.

The Box That Is Night

In the luminous house
evening diffuses from the center
so that walls with windows
lastly swoon

Under the spell
of vanishing light
I open the box
that is night

Inside I place
my father's spit and polish
my mother's elbow grease

To which I add
my surgical precision

any number of regrets

and this day's scuttlebutt

I heed a child's
faint request

leave the nightlight on

Picking Mushrooms

In the woods after rain
up on my father's shoulders
I point below at logs
and boulders, wet leaves
cold flick against my face
our breath expelled
in tandem as he walks

lingering raindrops
tap the forest floor

I hold a homemade
canvas bag
for the mushrooms
that we find

We step, then pause
and down I go
to pick some

and leave
the poison ones
behind

Sister Sun

There are three of us,
our bony selves
stand out especially
in summer.

Knocking ankle bones
we kick the covers
from the bed
each morning.

This day, one sister says,
will be a scorcher!

She rises,
limbs askew,
until with grace
she stretches
all the kinks of sleep,
into one long, slender reach.

Father On The Staircase
for Salvatore Torregrossa
You never sang your misery —Allen Ginsberg

You stare into the camera lens.
Your eyes are holes, your smile
barely there, coerced to sit

on the bottom steps
of the staircase in the hallway
in the old house on Roanoke Street.

So many photographs of us
standing there throughout the years
without you. On this day

we children all around you
strike a pose, like points on
a compass. On this day

love could not heal
whatever brought you
to exhaustion. If you had

asked me then I would have said
it was the pinched and ropey
scars on your shoulder

where bullets
hit their mark on the beach
in Normandy, D-Day plus Four

mother would say. You look to her,
she fills your eyes with light
as beautiful as pink peonies

that flourish underneath
the backyard cypress trees.
At her command—we smile

lift our arms above our heads
like rainbows, like angels
embracing air.

The Summer Tree

Fragile woody tangle
mock-orange overhang
of bower, fragrant shower
bright yellow pollen
petals like paper
satin white spray
green leaves
hum of bees
sunlight
knife-gray shade
fieldstone border
sticks and branches
twist, wistful child
sits in the humid warmth
mute as ants and clouds

Pool Play

the green glow undulates in the dark
a translucent lattice of water
                      waving us in

we take the air's weightless bud
                        into our mouths

slip into the glassy lime light
                      a slender splash
against the jasmine-scented night

entwine floating tendrils of hair
                      fingers, legs
breasts pressed
          in a calligraphy
               of desire

Meeting Saifra

Clearly, he was her son—
olive skin and espresso-brown
hair they both wore long.

Safira pulled hers back
in a low chignon
like the old Portuguese.

Dante turned to shove
the untrued door shut.
Just a few steps
in the small kitchen
brought us close.

Mamae, he said,
this is my girlfriend.

The fevered heat
of a frenzied mind
shone through her hazel eyes,
a deep line furrowed her brow.

Lamb of God, she said,
How's that you're not a boy?

Her words hung in the air
like a dash of cinnamon
in the *caldo verde*
simmering on the stove.

Safira put a finger to her lips.

At The Zócalo
    dedicated to Armondo 'Négro' Delgado

                    Sapo Leche whistles at doorways
                          calls out Jimmy, who
                                  always wears sandals, who

whistles in turn two
    houses down to call out
        Négro   they go

                                downtown
                              to whistle at girls
                         who strut by the fountain

and there   can you see?
    Tía is watching
                                rosy red tanagers

                    fly through the cool spray

        whistling

La Fuente Dulce

I have built a grand passionate fountain
in my zócalo heart
where black-braided women rendezvous
with blue and white mockingbirds.
Leaves ruffle in a tropical breeze,
los holanes de una falda,
amid the twitter of romance and song.

I laid the tile for you, in pieces, *con cuidado,*
a mano, pressed the gritty, soft grout
around a colorful glass mosaic
mirror of sky and sea;
the green flora of Guatemalan hillsides
rose-colored clouds *de una tierra Antigua*
purple smoke from a rumbling volcano
and the dark brown of everyone's eyes.

I rise with the scent of you,
oh sweet one, from the center
naked in the sparkling play
of a fountain I have built for you.

Her Earrings
for Elaine

Little planets dangle
from her ears, soft
puffy lobes of pink
that wrangle beads of sun
and silver glint of glass,
she turns, and talks
a foreign tongue,
they swing
and then her
fingers move
into her hair,
long and straight
to swish it
lightly.

Night Thyme
for Nina

The silver heart above her heart
flickers like a silent film
in the fading light

*Are dreams like movies
behind my eyes
when I sleep?*
she asks

her lashes are curls
of jasmine
filigreed
against her pillow

I have big dreams
she murmurs

her black hair disappears
into long shadows

evening primrose
press at windows
night phlox
opens to the moon

Bus Route After The Fires
    for Mynor

You can smell fire in the rain,
burnt dirt and smoke. Drizzle
wets hair, beads on eyelashes—
blink and the mountains slide.

Charcoal sticks push
through ash like the stubble
of a five o'clock shadow.
Soil turns to mud, steers
around stumps and boulders,
merges with debris, twists
down gullies and canyons.

Below—the city streets are lined
with a white skirt of concrete slabs.

School kids, right on time,
wait for the yellow bus
chugging up hilly roads.
Bus driver hurries them on,
glancing every few minutes
at the bald, gray foothills
slipping in the rain.

Undedicated Street

In the doldrums of this winter afternoon
shadows stretch across the road,
its surface cracked like veins on skin.

Loose gravel skitters on asphalt
when each solitary car speeds by
like a black-footed cat on the run.

I hear rustling palm fronds, the growl of a low-flying plane.
Somewhere a wrought iron gate clangs shut.
Dogs bark. A lone bird trills in the eucalyptus tree.

Grass tips bristle, their silhouettes fan out on cold cement.
Long, low sunrays finger mailboxes that gleam like mushrooms
in the shifting light.

Doors here are motionless.

Searching past the pulse that beats in my throat, I listen
for your ageless whisper

find it silent.

Avvoltoi

There was a poem in the air,
three blackbirds sailing,
big as grackles but more
graceful. Three of them

not far, not high, just over
the house, flying around and
round again. *Like those birds,*
Emily says, *who circle around
something dead or dying.*

I can see the feathered edge of wide
wing tips, think *carrion* but don't
say it because our conversation
is not a crossword puzzle.

Hawks, I say instead
And Melanie asks,
*What do you think is dead
over there?* Which makes
Santos and Destiny stop their
page-turning and look up

at three black birds
soaring on invisible currents.

Angel's Mother
    for poet Angel Garcia

Is she still waiting for that train, Angel?
Where you left her? Where she's waiting?
All around her have grown tall trees.

They built a four-lane highway and now
the tracks are rusted. I don't see her face.
She wears a coat. I think it's blue.

Only you know, Angel. You put her there.
Made us believe she'd walked there by herself.
Has determination become despair by now?

Or does she see way down the road a destination
of the heart? Her sons, or maybe just the sunrise,
so beautiful she stays to watch the pale light turn gold.

Nixtamal

She snaps a kitchen towel
at the brood of hens and chicks
that strut near the table in the yard.

Having cleaned the *maíz*
of pebbles and bits of stalk
she rattles grit-addled flint in a sieve.

She kneels by a heavy stone *metate*
grinding field corn into tiny bees
her hands pound and roll the kernels

with a long, black *mano*. Intent
as watching rain fall, she guides
the pestle's spark against the grain.

A fine golden powder rises up
like a dust plume after *un temblor,*
clings to the soft hairs on her arms.

She sweeps the cornmeal
with a stiff straw brush,
piles it high into a blue enamel dish.

Her daughter's small complaint
from yesterday, her husband's firm
determined plans *para mañana*

winnow like wheat from the chaff.

A yellow sun shines in her bowl.

Desert Crossing
A witness narrative from the US/Mexico border

The story is told by her husband
so young himself, barely a man,
how he must have loved her

the girl with the shell necklace.

They walked and walked
together, they cried their love
for each other, he cried
his tears into her mouth.

When she faltered, he held her,
he pushed her and dragged her
                          and carried her
under the fire of stars in the night.

They prayed their love
together, delirious

a real girl, with black wavy hair
her mother braided the day they left,
a promise to take care of each other
in her wide and happy smile.

He sobs and sobs as the camera rolls
clutching the image of his one true love

the girl with the white shell necklace.

Day Laborer

The hot sun at mid-day
is not as yellow
as the sun of my home.

A single thin palm
in the span of concrete
bends like a finger pointing the way.

In the soot on the sidewalk
at the bus stops of LA
I look for the bus that scrolls HOME.

A hummingbird
hovers at eye level
wants me to follow
but I cannot fly.

The sand in the lot
by the tire shop
is like cornmeal shushing
from cloth sacks in my
mother's kitchen.

I stand very still
in the cool morning air
against a cinder block wall
hands in the pockets
of my sweatshirt
splattered with paint.

Selling Candy

Selling candy outside
the Washington Mutual
is not working out,
the boy tells me, hunched
in layers of clothes like
he's waiting for the school
bus on a cold morning,
shoulders like a wire
coat hanger, face tanned
by the winter sun.

He lies about the soccer team
to customers lined up at the ATM
who clutch their cash
in the holiday rush home
to *buñuelos* and tamales.
He plies *Raisinets* in a box—two bucks.

Candy labels look like crayons
stacked inside the cardboard carton.
I take whatever he gives me,
hand over three bills—two ones and a five.

Use it for bus fare, I say.

He bends and slips the five into his sneaker.

Uncle Lowell And His Niece Play Hide And Secret
for Faith

He collapses above me
and doesn't leave
until daylight's mighty
muscle moves the
ton of shadow
that plasters
my chest
to the floorboards
under the bed

without looking

I know he is drunk
I can smell him
from inside the wicker
laundry basket
his frothy whisper
a freight train in my ears

like a tornado

his bellow
rips
through the garage
where I wait it out
in the narrow crevice
between the washing machine
and dryer

Rendezvous

In the crowded parking lot—two cars.

I'm guessing the woman
in her black leather boots,
gray pencil skirt and cardigan
directs a program for...
gifted child musicians.

The man wears a business suit.

They stand apart having just
stepped out of their respective
vehicles. She drives a silver Lexus.
He drives a blue Mercedes. Their
eyes lock in conversation
barely blinking, never looking down
at keys or wristwatch. She nods.

He slides back into the driver's seat,
leans over to open the passenger
door. She tosses her shoulder length
blond hair and looks around,

catches my eye before getting in.

Neighbors

The misdirected letter is returned
to the neighbor's curbside box.
The short metal tongue that
bleats like a goat when opened
is slammed shut. The pit bulls

pant, lethargic in the summer
heat, the sky is quiet but for
the droning of a mourning dove.

The pit bulls wag their stumpy
tails, nudge their noses
through the wrought iron gate.

I rub my knuckles against
their knuckled heads and coo
good doggie—kissing ass
just in case some day
some incongruity
rankles their brindled
pit bull brains.

Old Dogs

lead me at odd hours
outside, sometimes
the neighbors are awake
their lights on,
sometimes asleep; me too
at the door in my nightclothes.

A freight train whistle
yowls, diffused by distance,
a radio plays a Mexican ballad,
I can smell the wood smoke
from a bonfire next door,
hear logs sizzle,
break apart in the pit

I imagine sparks.

A clothes dryer spins
the rhythmic click
of buttons on Levis 501's.
The boys slouch in English,
low tones indistinguishable.

The father's voice is deep
and carries through the night.

He says in Spanish

"*Mijo*, try these plums, *qué rico.*"

The Bullet In His Head

is so small that no one
knows it's there
but him.

He rubs his neck behind his ear
out of habit and often
doesn't sleep well.

When it's cold outside
inside his skull
feels cold, too.

He walks and drives and works each day
with a bullet in his head.

Sometimes he drinks too much
and argues with his parents,
his girlfriend.

They try to tell him all the things
they have learned from life.
I've heard him say

That's alright for you but you're not me.

You don't have a bullet in your head.

Our Cemetery

has no cypress trees

no sundial, no overgrowth
of forest at its edge

Our cemetery has a chain link fence
a fanciful wrought iron arch
facing a busy street

Darkness does not descend
on this patch of sacred land

we have street lights

There is no chapel, no stained
    glass window, no map
        on a pedestal

you will never lose your way

We are buried on an archipelago
of grass and gravestones

where small American flags
just seem to appear
each Memorial Day

The city grows up around us
a muffler shop, the Diamante Bar
Hong Kong-style Chinese Food to-go

and still we are laid down

Once in a while a commuter
waiting at the red light notices

a freshly dug hole
and a wreath of flowers

Mary Torregrossa is a storyteller and, most importantly, a *story-listener*, a practice she has honed in her job as an ESL teacher in Southern California. Originally from Providence, Rhode Island, a place she revisits in life and in poetry, she blends a diversity of people, places and experiences from both coasts into her poetry.

Torregrossa's poems also appear in *Bearing the Mask: Southwestern Persona Poems* and *Wide Awake: Poets of Los Angeles and Beyond*. Her work is included in *Voices From Leimert Park Redux*, an anthology of "observers and keepers of culture" from the famous World Stage in Los Angeles. Individual poems are part of the *Poems of Arrival* project, an art installation by ShinPei Takeda at the New Americans Museum in San Diego, and in Poet Laureate Juan Felipe Herrera's *Poems of Unity*, as well as *Lament For The Dead*, an on-line project honoring victims of gun violence.

Torregrossa is a winner of the Arroyo Arts Collective *Poetry In The Windows* community event and named Newer Poet of Los Angeles XIV by the prestigious Los Angeles Poetry Festival. Her work has been published in *Like A Girl, Lummox,* and *The Altadena Poetry Review*, among others and on the websites for *East Jasmine Review, Moonday, poeticdiversity, Writers At Work, Rhode Island Roads* and the *Colorado Blvd.* on-line magazine.